ONLINE INVESTIGATIONS:

Skype

CI Publishing derives material from active-duty law enforcement officers and instructors with years of experience in the subject matter. The authors of ONLINE INVESTIGATIONS: Facebook chose to remain anonymous as they.are prevented from disclosing their identities for operational security reasons and due to departmental policies regarding attribution and endorsements.

FIRST EDITION

CI PUBLISHING

ONLINE INVESTIGATIONS: Skype
© 2015 by CI Publishing. All rights reserved.

Books may be purchased in bulk or using a government purchase order by contacting the publisher at:

CI Publishing
4695 Chabot Drive Suite 200, Pleasanton, CA 94588
Publisher: CI Publishing
Editor: Elizabeth Peterson
1. Law Enforcement 2. Investigations 3. Social Media
First Edition
Printed in the United States of America

Contents

Introduction

Skype is a communications application that provides voice and video calls using computers, tablets, and mobile phones via the internet. Skype users can also send instant messages, exchange images and files, send video messages, and have conference calls. Skype is available for the Windows, Mac, Android, Blackberry, iOS, and Windows Phone smartphones and tablets.

The availability of inexpensive calls, international capability, and the capacity to be used on devices other than a phone make it an attractive method of communication. The same reasons Skype is popular with law abiding citizens makes it attractive to criminals who make use of Skype to commit crimes and to communicate.

Understanding Skype and the data the company retains is an essential element of any investigations; particularly international investigations. Approximately one-third of all international calls are made using Skype.

Identifying Skype Accounts

Identifying Skype phone numbers can be difficult. But once located, the quantity and quality of information stored by the company makes investigating Skype worth the effort.

Skype uses a Voice Over Internet Protocol (VOIP) system to transmit calls and data. Most Skype users are aware they are communicating via the service such as when using video chat. However, it can be difficult to determine if a received call is from a Skype application. As an example of the difficulty in identifying Skype calls, a user can make a call or text using the Skype application using their real mobile phone number which appears in the caller ID of the receiving device. However, the call detail records from the cellular service provider will not show a call made from the suspect's device. This is because they did not use the cellular service provider to make the call, they used Skype. Similarly, forensic examination of a suspect's mobile device will not show any outgoing activity in the call logs as the call was made using the Skype application and not the native calling feature of the device.

Adding to the difficulty of investigating Skype numbers is the challenge of Skype's trunked numbers. It may take as long as 24 hours to display a new user's Skype caller ID. Phone calls and text messages made during that time will display and generic trunk number such as 661-748-0240 or 661-748-0241. These phone numbers are general outgoing phone numbers and can be simultaneously associated with thousands of different users.

Additionally, Skype users are able to pick a phone number to be displayed on the caller ID of a receiving phone. These numbers can be from any geographical area in the United States.

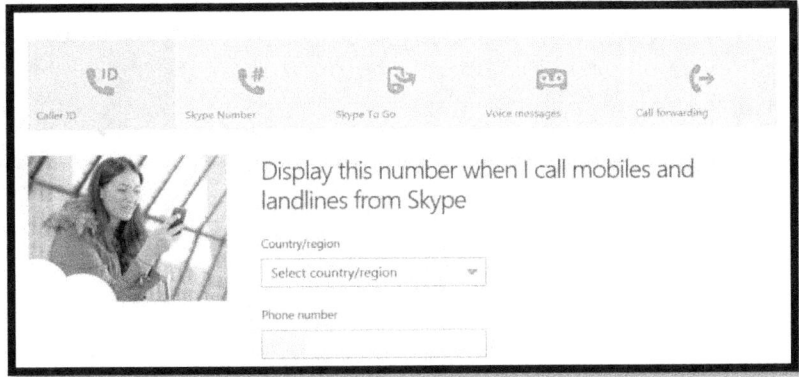

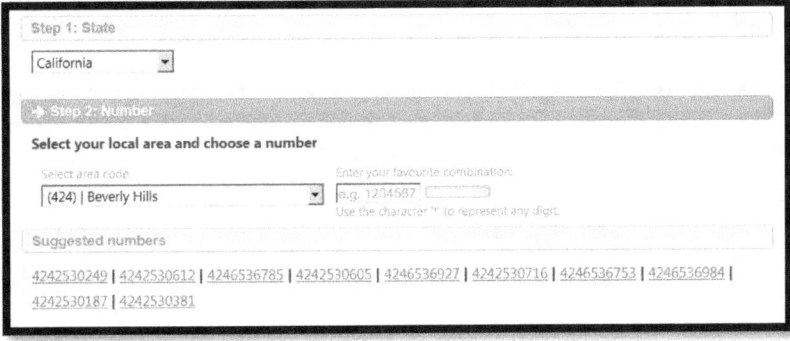

Why You May Be Missing Outgoing International Calls

Many organized crime investigations involve associating a suspect in the United States with their counterparts in a foreign country. Traditionally, international phone numbers were easy to spot in the call detail records of the suspect's phone number. Unfortunately, Skype makes it very difficult to identify outgoing international phone numbers.

Skype users have the option of making international calls using a local access number. Once they contact the local access number there are a series of voice prompts that allow them to complete the international call. However, the call detail records of the suspect will only reveal the local access number and not the international phone number they called. A Skype user may enter the phone number they will be calling from to make the international call.

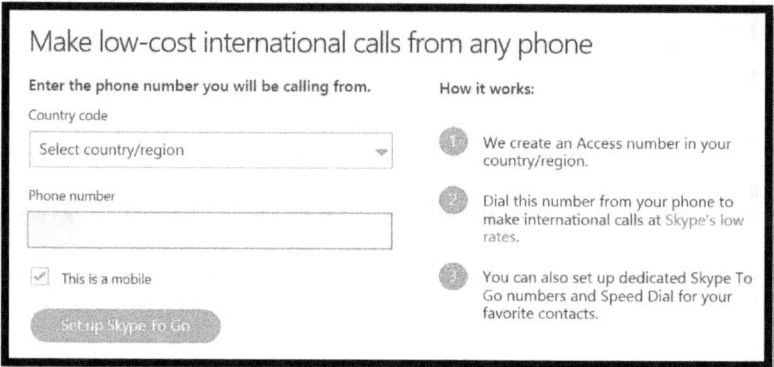

Once established customers are assigned the local access number. To make an international call using Skype the customer calls the local access number and then the call is routed to the country of origin.

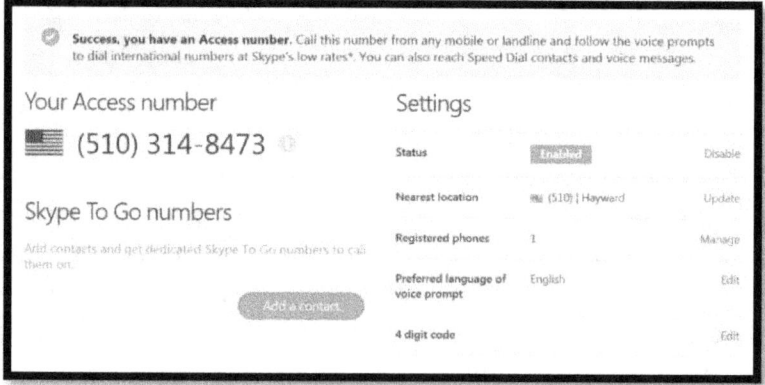

Investigators may see the calling activity to the access number but researching it does not show any indication it is Skype international access number. In this example, the initial investigation shows the phone number is a Sprint mobile phone from one free online service and Level 3 Communications from another online service.

Area Code	Prefix	City/Switch Name (Click for city search)	State/Prov. Area Map	Telephone Company Web link	Telco Type
510	314	HAYWARD	California	SPRINT SPECTRUM L.P.	PCS

Results

Forms and Records Requests enabled with ZetX Account

Number	Wireless Number?	Carrier	Carrier Contact Number
15103148473	No	Level 3 Communications, LLC	☎ 918-547-9611

When confronted with a possible Skype number many law enforcement investigators use free or paid online services to determine the provider of cellular or landline telephone services. Unfortunately, these techniques do not work well with investigations involving Skype. Public records databases will reveal the underlying cellular service provider but they will not reveal any associated Skype account.

Many public records databases and law enforcement databases will show a phone number associated with a Skype investigation as being serviced by Bandwidth.com LLC. In fact, the majority of phone numbers examined in the pool of available Skype numbers for new customers show most of them are listed to this company.

Skype and Bandwidth.com

Voice Over Internet Providers (VOIP) such as Skype can be a particularly challenging subset of phone technology to work with. The fact is, checking phone numbers with VOIP service usually results in incorrect information. For example, zetx.com is one of the more widely used phone number lookup services. Entering a phone number, such as 424-253-0249, using this online search tool shows the phone number is assigned to Bandwidth.com LLC in Beverley Hills. Unfortunately, the number is actually a Skype number and attempts to serve Bandwidth.com LLC with legal process will be fruitless and may cause unnecessary delays during a critical incident.

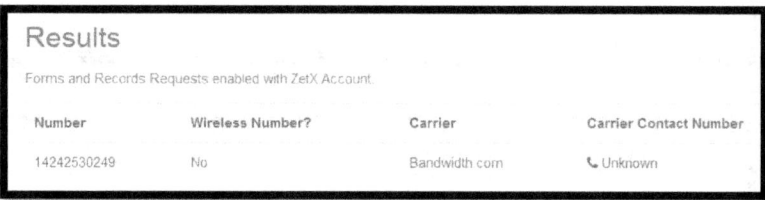

Bandwidth.com LLC is a leading provider of business and residential VOIP services under the name Republic Wireless. It also resells services, including blocks of phone numbers, to other providers. Skype, Google Voice, Magic Jack, and Vonnage are some of the most commonly encountered VOIP providers where the initial records check indicates the number belongs to Bandwidth.com LLC.

Likely due to the large number of law enforcement inquires the company receives, Bandwidth.com LLC has established certain protocols and procedures for routine and emergency inquiries. The company will release the underlying service provider to requesting law enforcement agencies without a subpoena, court order, or search warrant. Bandwidth.com will only release information about whether the phone number is serviced by their Republic Wireless brand or has been leased or sold to another provider such as Skype, Google Voice, Magic Jack, or Vonnage.

Routine inquiries can be sent via email and addressed to:

BANDWIDTH.COM LLC
Contact: Custodian of Records
900 Main Campus Drive, Suite 500, Raleigh, North Carolina 27606
Fax Number: 919-238-9903
Email: legal@bandwidth.com

For exigent circumstances, such as a barricaded suspect, bomb threat, or kidnapping, during normal business hours law enforcement officers may send an exigent circumstances request to the company at legal@bandwidth.com. All exigent circumstances requests must be initiated in writing via email. If there is not a prompt response, or if the emergency situation is afterhours, law enforcement officers may contact the fiduciary company that handles these situations on behalf of Bandwidth.com LLC. The fiduciary company is Neustar and may be reached at 877-510-4357. Select option one and advise the Neustar representative you are inquiring about a number assigned to Bandwidth.com LLC. Both companies will only provide a law enforcement officer with the name of the company who the phone number was assigned to. Further information regarding the subscriber, call records, or any other information can only be obtained from the company who provides service to the assigned phone number. Bandwidth.com LLC and Neustar do not have the information to provide and can only determine what company the phone number is assigned to.

What Information Does Skype Have?

Unlike other VoIP providers, it is difficult for a criminal to use Skype anonymously. In order to establish an account and use Skype, a customer has to provide a fair amount of personal information.

Identifying Information

Skype requires user to provide identification information in order to use the service. This includes name, which could be false, but the true name can be located via other means listed below, a user name selected by the customer, address, telephone number, mobile number, and email address. Skype does not accept other VOIP numbers such as Google Voice during the account registration process so associated phone numbers are likely to be legitimate. While it is possible to use 'burner' email addresses and phone numbers when establishing the account, completing the Skype set up requires additional information which can lead to the user's true identity.

Profile Information

A Skype user may create a profile including age, gender, country of residence, language preference, and other optional information for public display. All of this user supplied information could be false.

Internet Protocol (IP) Addresses

Skype collects and stores electronic identification data including the Internet Protocol (IP) address of the devices used to access the service. If you are going to investigate a case involving Skype, you must understand IP addresses and how to examine them.

Every device involved in communicating on the internet uses an IP address. IP addresses come in two versions IPv4 and IPv6. IPv4 addresses consist of 4 numbers ranging from 0 to 255, separated by periods.

$$110.311.148.31$$

The total number of variations of IPv4 addresses is roughly 4.3 billion. With the explosion of the internet, personal computers, laptops, tablets, cell phones, and wearable technology the number of IPv4 addresses is insufficient to meet the anticipated demand. IPv6 addresses were developed to increase the pool of available numbers. IPv6 addresses have eight groups of four alphanumeric characters separated by colons. An example of a full IPv6 address is:

$$FE80:0000:0000:0000:0202:B3FF:FE1E:8329$$

An IPv6 address may be collapses to shorten the total number of characters. An example of a collapsed IPv6 addresses is:

$$FE80::0202:B3FF:FE1E:8329$$

The consecutive colons (::) notation is used to represent four successive blocks that contain all zeros.

Computers and other devices may be assigned an IPv4 or IPv6 internet protocol address by an internet service provider. An internet service provider (ISP) is usually a commercial vendor providing service but may also be a business or government organization. They may reserve or be assigned block of IPv4 addresses that are assigned to their users. An IPv4 address can roughly be compared to a phone number assigned to a particular device. Unfortunately, it can get complicated as there are three types of IPv4 addresses:

Static-IP addresses are permanently assigned to devices. An entity, such as craigslist, maintaining a constant presence on the internet usually requires a static IP address.

Dynamic-IP addresses are temporarily assigned from a pool of available addresses registered to an ISP. These addresses area assigned to a computer or mobile device when as user begins an online session. A dynamic IP address may vary from one logon session to the next.

Semi-Dynamic-These IP addresses are technically dynamic but may be assigned to a particular device for a prolonged period of time.

Tracing IP Addresses

You can learn a lot of information by examining the IP addresses, including which internet service provider (ISP) the user is using. In some cases this may be the user's company (e.g. Ford.com). In other cases it may be just one of the large ISPs such as ATT or Comcast. It is also possible to determine the approximate physical location of the user (e.g. Palo Alto, California.)

There are many free website to trace an IP address. For way of illustration, the following images are from whatismyipaddress.com. The information from each publicly available website is identical so it often a matter of user preference for an interface.

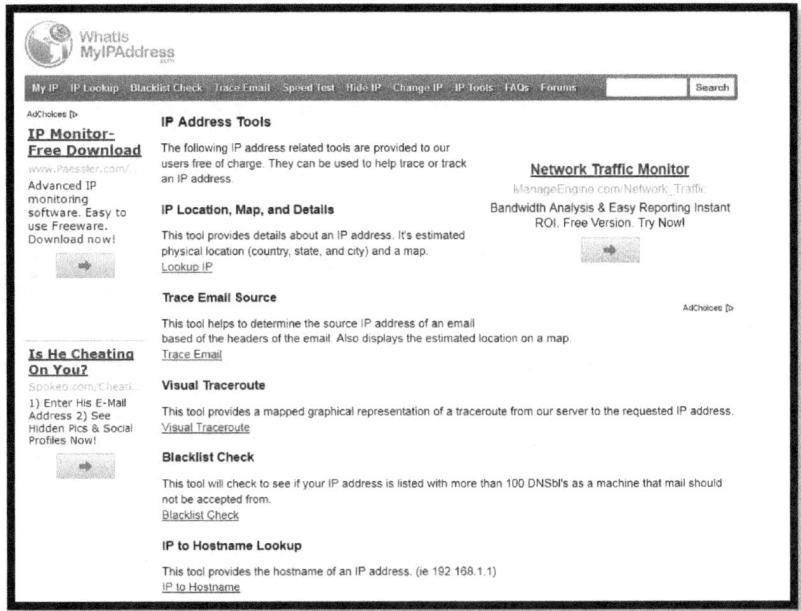

To trace an IP address, first copy the originating IP address from the email you are interested in. Next go to whichever website you are going to use to trace the IP address. In this case, from the whatismyipaddress.com website, click on the blue link that says Lookup IP.

IP Location, Map, and Details

This tool provides details about an IP address. It's estimated physical location (country, state, and city) and a map.
Lookup IP

Clicking the link will bring up the screen below.

Lookup IP Address Location

These details include the hostname, Geographic location information (includes country, region/state, city, latitude, longitude and telephone area code.), and a location specific map.

Geolocation technology can never be 100% accurate in providing the location of an IP address. When the IP address is a proxy server and it does not expose the user's IP address it is virtually impossible to locate the user. The country accuracy is estimated at about 99%. For IP addresses in the United States, it is 90% accurate on the state level, and 81% accurate within a 25 mile radius. Our world-wide users indicate 55% accurate within 25km.

Please enter the IP address you want to lookup below:

70.199.87.91	Lookup IP Address

The website will automatically bring up the public information about the IP address. You will see a lot of information is available including the ISP provider (Verizon Wireless) and the general geographic location (Tracy, CA).

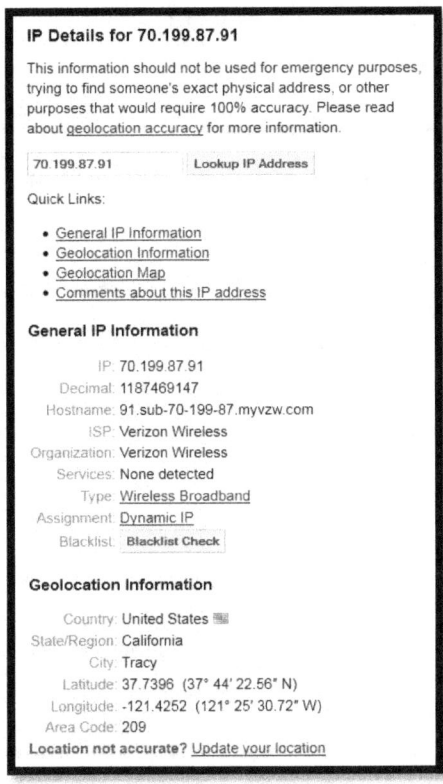

IP Details for 70.199.87.91

This information should not be used for emergency purposes, trying to find someone's exact physical address, or other purposes that would require 100% accuracy. Please read about geolocation accuracy for more information.

| 70.199.87.91 | Lookup IP Address |

Quick Links:

- General IP Information
- Geolocation Information
- Geolocation Map
- Comments about this IP address

General IP Information

IP: 70.199.87.91
Decimal: 1187469147
Hostname: 91.sub-70-199-87.myvzw.com
ISP: Verizon Wireless
Organization: Verizon Wireless
Services: None detected
Type: Wireless Broadband
Assignment: Dynamic IP
Blacklist: Blacklist Check

Geolocation Information

Country: United States
State/Region: California
City: Tracy
Latitude: 37.7396 (37° 44' 22.56" N)
Longitude: -121.4252 (121° 25' 30.72" W)
Area Code: 209
Location not accurate? Update your location

The results of tracing the IP address will reveal the Internet Service Provider (ISP), the organization name if the IP address is assigned to a business or government organization, whether the IP address is dynamic or static, and some general location data.

Financial Information

Skype is not free. Using the service requires an initial purchase of credits or a recurring payment. Fees are required to make phone calls and text messages, to display another caller ID number, and to use an international number for others to contact the Skype user without incurring international rates. In order to pay for Skype, a customer has to use a credit card or an electronic payment system such as PayPal.

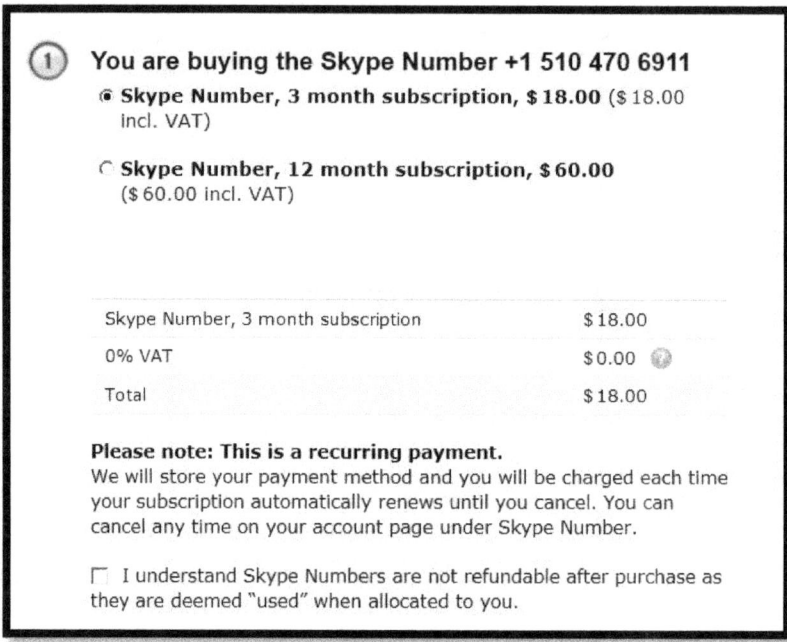

The requirement to provide billing information is the Achilles Heel for criminals using Skype. The personal and profile information a suspect used to create the account will not work during the billing process. To actually use the service the suspect needs to provide a legitimate and verified method of payment. This includes the name and billing address on any credit cards used for the service.

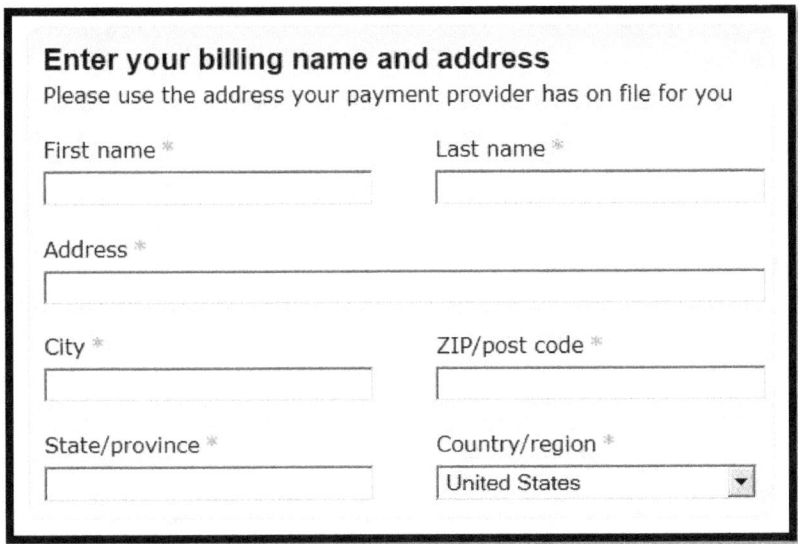

Enter your billing name and address

Please use the address your payment provider has on file for you

First name *

Last name *

Address *

City *

ZIP/post code *

State/province *

Country/region *

United States

Payments to Skype can be made using a variety of options including credit cards and online payment providers. Each method of payment provides additional investigative leads. These leads may require additional legal process to obtain relevant information.

Select your payment method

VISA   MasterCard   PayPal   Skrill moneybookers

PayByCash   AMERICAN EXPRESS   JCB   paysafe

CARTE BLEUE

If the suspect used a Visa, MasterCard, or American Express card to pay for Skype it will be necessary to determine the issuing bank for subsequent follow-up. The first six digits of a credit or debit card are known as the Bank Identification Number or BIN. All Visa cards begin with the number 4. MasterCards begin with the numbers 51 through 55. American Express cards begin with the number 37.

Determining the issuing bank for Visa and MasterCard may be done check online. There are a number of free online services to check a BIN and determine the issuing bank. Two examples, include www.bindb.com and www.binlist.net. Both are free and only require the first six digits of the credit card to determine the issuing bank.

The website www.bindb.com limits their free look up to ten queries from a single computer or network.

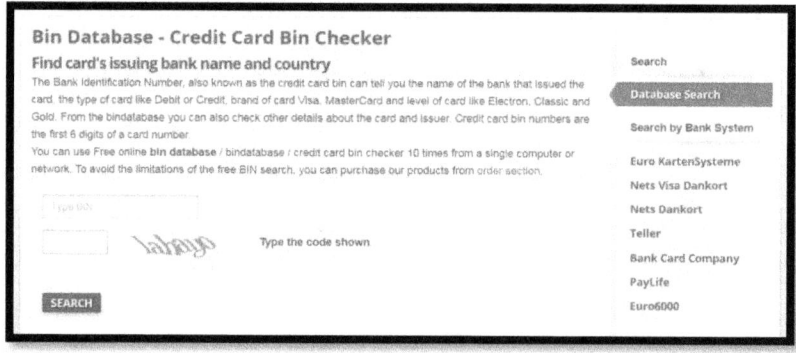

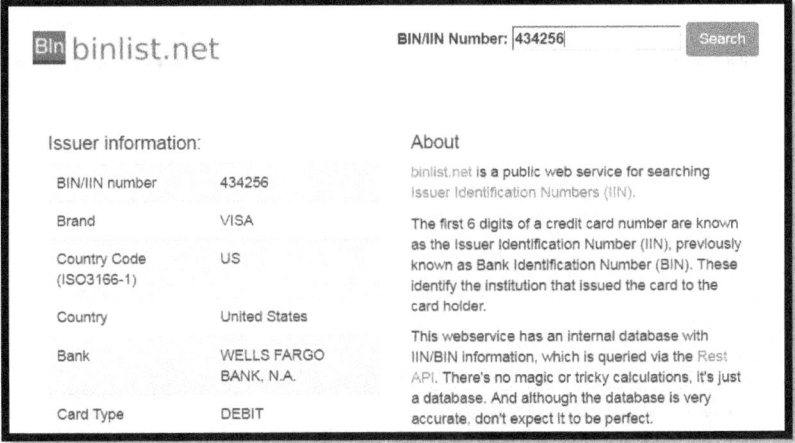

Bin:	414720
Card Brand:	VISA
Issuing Bank:	JPMORGAN CHASE BANK N.A.
Card Type:	CREDIT
Card Level:	CLASSIC
Iso Country Name:	UNITED STATES
Iso Country A2:	US
Iso Country A3:	USA
Iso Country Number:	840
Bank's website:	www.jpmorganchase.com
Customer Care Line:	1-800-935-9935
Bank Address:	******** [?] Available on Ultimate Database
Formal Bank:	******** [?] Available on Ultimate Database
Additional Info:	1-800-935-9935 OR 1-800-432-3117 OR 1-302-594-8200 OR www.chase.com

The other site, www.binlist.com does not have any restrictions on the number of times it may be used.

Bln binlist.net

BIN/IIN Number: 434256   [Search]

Issuer information:

BIN/IIN number	434256
Brand	VISA
Country Code (ISO3166-1)	US
Country	United States
Bank	WELLS FARGO BANK, N.A.
Card Type	DEBIT

About

binlist.net is a public web service for searching Issuer Identification Numbers (IIN).

The first 6 digits of a credit card number are known as the Issuer Identification Number (IIN), previously known as Bank Identification Number (BIN). These identify the institution that issued the card to the card holder.

This webservice has an internal database with IIN/BIN information, which is queried via the Rest API. There's no magic or tricky calculations, it's just a database. And although the database is very accurate, don't expect it to be perfect.

Once the issuing bank has been determined it will be necessary to locate the proper legal compliance department to send additional legal process to. Many bank subpoena compliance departments can be found using a major search engine such as Google. However, the results can sometime be confusing or contradictory. One method for locating law enforcement subpoena compliance contact information is the database found at www.search.org/isp-list.

The website is hosted by SEARCH, The National Consortium for Justice Information and Statistics. It is a nonprofit organization that performs research and training in a variety of topics. One of the resources they make available is the ISP list. The ISP list was originally designed as a place for law enforcement officers to share contact information for internet service providers (ISPs.) However, the list has grown to expand a number of other types of businesses including cell phone service providers, email providers, rental car companies, and financial institutions. The website is a good starting point as it lists the contact information for a specific business and the last time that information was updated.

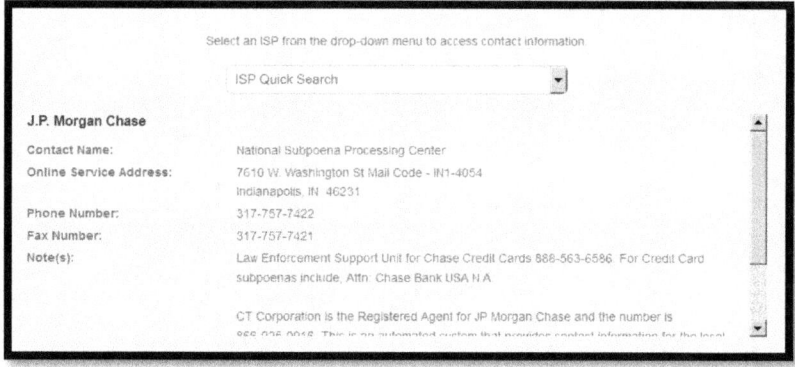

If the suspect used PayPal as their payment processor there is additional information available via legal process. PayPal is able to supply law enforcement investigators with their customer's name, address, phone number(s), Social Security number, the IP address used by the customer every time they log in, linked financial accounts and credit cards, transaction history, and any prior complaints against the user.

The other methods of payment available to Skype customers include international processors such as Japan Credit Bureau (JCB) and the United Kingdrom based Skrill. All of these payment processors are from countries that either have specific treaties with the United States to cooperate in law enforcement investigations or they are signatories to the Mutual Legal Assistance Treaty (MLAT.) To serve these companies with a search warrant, court order, or subpoena it may be necessary to involve the Legal Attaché Office of the Federal Bureau of Investigation. The Legal Attaché Office can assist with navigating the process of serving international legal process.

It is common for local law enforcement investigators to not investigate cases involving international payment processors. This may be due to a belief there are jurisdictional issues or that these companies will not honor legal process from the United States. This is an incorrect assumption and deprives the investigator of a potential gold mine of information. For example, the payment processor Skrill collects the following information which can be obtained with a search warrant:

- Customer name, address, email address, telephone number, date of birth, and bank or payment card details.
- Transactional details, including credit and debit card history.
- Bank account details including account holder, account name, account number, and transaction history.
- Internet protocol address, log-in dates and time, operating system, and web browser type.

All of this information is lost if an investigator does not serve the foreign payment processor.

System Information

Skype collects information about their customer's usage and interaction with the software and service and can provide the computer platform and operating system, mobile device type and operating system, web browser type, Skype Wi-Fi enabled hotspot use, and calling destinations.

Contacts

Skype users have the ability to import contacts and related data from linked email and social media accounts. This information, as well as the source of the contact data, can be obtained from Skype.

Traffic Data

In order to process billing information Skype maintains data about the duration of calls, the number of text messages sent or received, the originating number, and the terminating number. These records are similar to call detail records from phone companies.

Content of Instant Messages, Voice Messages, and Video Messages

Skype stores communications made using their service including instant messages (IM), voice, and video. This includes any media the user shares through the messaging services such as pictures, videos, and map location. These messages are generally stored between 30-90 days unless they are preserved. Specific preservation language and a sample template can be found in the Legal Process chapter.

Location Information

Skype obtains location information from the user's device and from the cellular service provider when a customer used mapping or location services. For example, if a user searches for Skype Wi-Fi access points, Skype collects the location information of the mobile device in order to show the customer's location in relation to those access points. Similarly, the company maintains location information if a user shares their location in a Skype message with another user. This location information may be derived from cell site, Global Positioning System (GPS) data, and Wi-Fi hot spots.

Mobile Device Information
This data includes a customer's mobile device type, manufacturer name, model number, operating system, and cellular service provider.

Wi-Fi Location/Connection Data
Skype records and stores location information based on the Wi-Fi networks a user connects to. When a customer connects to an open or password protected Wi-Fi network this information is recorded by Skype. These Wi-Fi networks can provide additional location information with additional legal process to the Wi-Fi access point service provider.

Social Media and Other Linked Accounts
Skype users can link social media accounts, such as Facebook, LinkedIn, or Twitter to import contact information. Once located, these social media providers can be targets for additional legal process to obtain additional information.

Many investigators are aware Skype is owned by Microsoft. However, they forget that this relationship means that a Skype user may also have a Microsoft account. Formerly known as a Windows Live ID or Microsoft Passport, the Microsoft account allows users to sign into the company's products, web sites, and services.

Even though Skype is a Microsoft product, the Microsoft account may have information that is not present in Skype. When a user creates a Microsoft account they provide an email address which is verified by the company, an alternate email address for password recovery, and a phone number.

Additional demographic information may be found in the Microsoft account including gender, country, date of birth, and zip code. This information may be the same or different as the user supplied profile information in the Skype account.

The Microsoft account retains system information in addition to the data retained by Skype. This includes a unique credential number, the user's IP address, web browser information, login dates and times, device manufacturer and model, and software version.

There may be linked accounts such as email services provided by outlook.com, live.com, hotmail.com, or msn.com. There may also be connected social networks such as Facebook, Twitter, and LinkedIn that are associated with the Microsoft account but not the Skype account.

Recovering Skype Message and Log Files From Computers and Mobile Devices

Traditional call details logs of communications between Skype users do not exist. To obtain messages, call logs, and videos made between Skype users it may be necessary to seize the computer or mobile device used to access Skype to recover them.

Skype messages and log files should always be recovered by a properly trained and equipped forensic technician whenever possible. However, a forensic technician is not always available to recover these types of files. Some law enforcement agencies do not have access to a forensic examiner or the turnaround time is so long it makes submitting a computer for examination useless. There are also situations where the need to recover data promptly outweighs the time required to recover the data in a forensically sound manner such as an imminent threat to life.

Manual Searches

There are a number of methods for recovering Skype messages and log files without a forensic technician. The first is to have a cooperating witness or victim export and save their messages. To view a conversation history the user must sign into their Skype account. Conversations can be viewed under the **Contacts** or **Recent** tabs.

The conversation list is sorted by date, with the most recent conversation at the top of the list. If the relevant conversation does not appear in the **Recent** list, scroll to the bottom and select **Show earlier messages** to display a full list of conversations.

Specific keywords can be searched for within a conversation by selecting the **Control** + **F** combination.

Instant messages cannot be selectively deleted. It is possible to right-click the message and select **Remove Message** but this option is only available for a few minutes after sending/receiving the message. In order to delete a specific message the entire conversation history must be removed. Deleting the conversation history removes everything associated with the conversation. This includes:

- Instant messages
- Calls
- Voice messages
- Video messages
- Text messages
- Sent and received files

Most people will avoid deleting everything associated with a conversation because they may want to avoid the appearance of guilt by covering their tracks. They may also want to keep some of the other, non-incriminating conversations or files. If a suspect does delete an entire Skype conversation, it is still possible to recover the deleted files via a forensic examination.

A common alternative to deleting everything associated with a conversation is to hide the conversation. To conceal a conversation a user simply needs to go to the **Conversation** tab in the top bar of the main Skype window and select **Hide Conversation**.

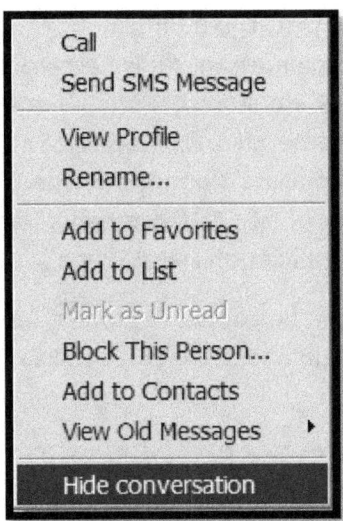

To view a hidden conversation, select the **View** tab at the top of the main Skype interface and then select **Show Hidden Conversations**. Any previously concealed conversations will not be visible in the main Skype window.

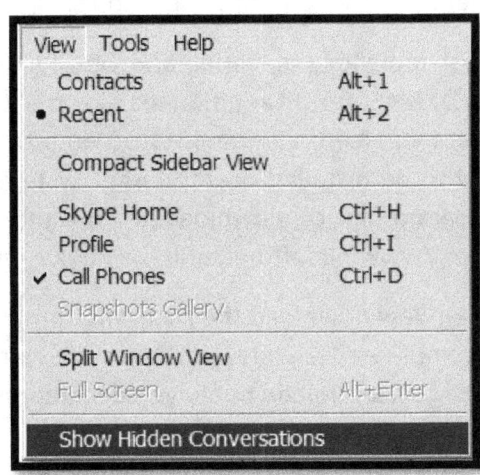

Preserving Skype Database Files

To preserve the Skype messages it is necessary to save the database file where they are stored. For computers using Windows Vista/7 the database file is located at **C:\Users\ windows_username\AppData\Roaming\Skype.** For Windows 8 the database is located at **C:\Documents and Settings\windows_username\Application Data\Skype**

The database file can be copied to storage media such as a USB drive or DVD. The database file can be examined later by a forensic technician.

Free, Automated Skype Recovery Tools

There are a number of software programs for recovering Skype messages and log files. Unfortunately, these tools are currently available only for computers and most do not meet the definition of a forensic tool. Investigating officers should be aware the use of non-forensic tools to recover Skype files could results in extended legal proceedings to ascertain the validity and the admissibility of evidence recovered using these tools.

One of the best tools for recovering and viewing Skype files is SkypeLogView by Nir Sofer. In addition to being free the software is also portable meaning it can be installed on a USB drive and does not need to be installed on the target system to recover data. The program can be downloaded from the developer's website at http://www.nirsoft.net/utils/skype_log_view.html.

To use SkypeLogView download the program from the web site. It comes in a compressed .zip file which must be extracted in order to use. For agencies that do not have a decompression utility, a free application called 7-Zip can be used to extract the files. 7-Zip is also portable so it can be installed without administrator rights from the department's information technology staff. Once the files are extracted they can be copied to a USB drive and used on a witness or suspect's computer.

Running the program is pretty self-explanatory. Double click the SkypeLogView icon to launch it.

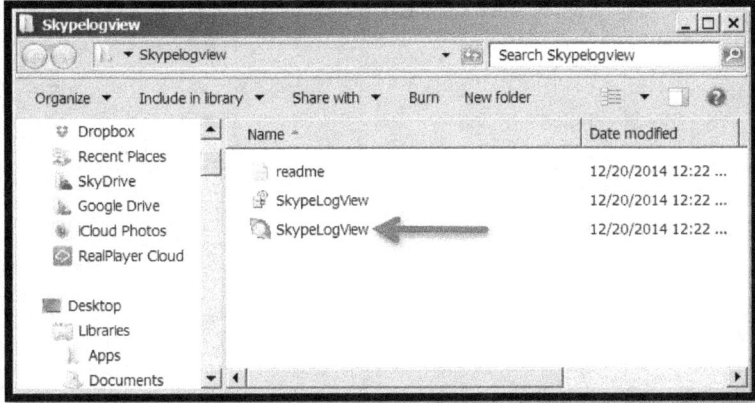

Select the appropriate user profile and press **OK**. SkypeLogView gives a user the option of only recovering data during a certain date/time range. In situations where the Skype account belongs to victim or cooperating witness it may be best to only download the relevant time frame.

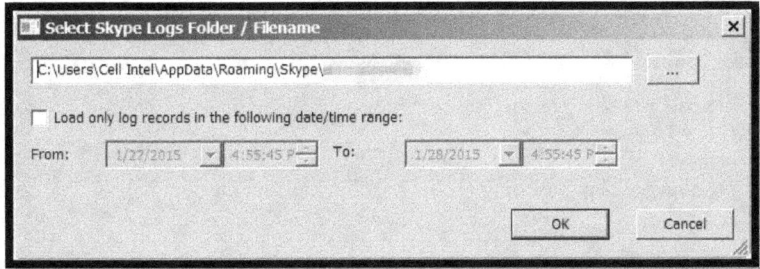

Once the profile is selected SkypeLogView automatically loads all message and log files.

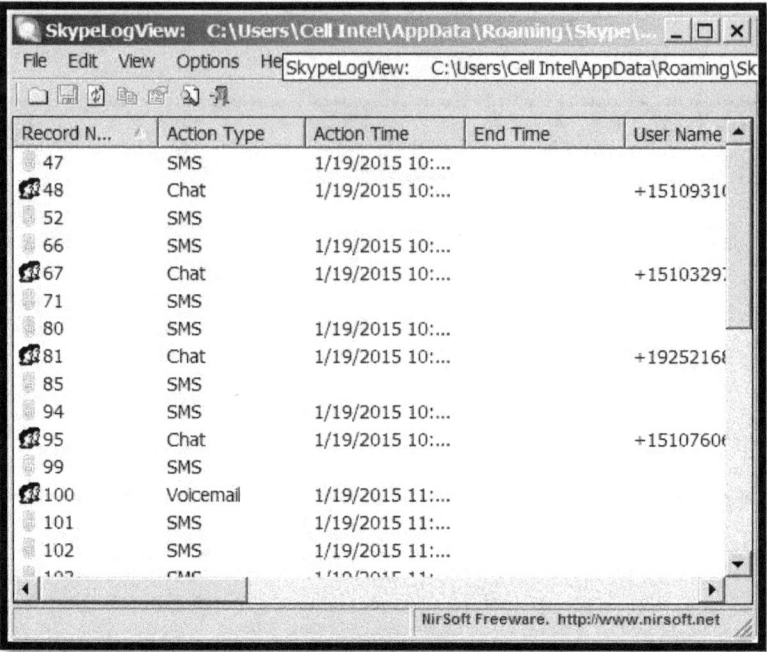

Double clicking an individual log, message, or chat brings up the details of the activity.

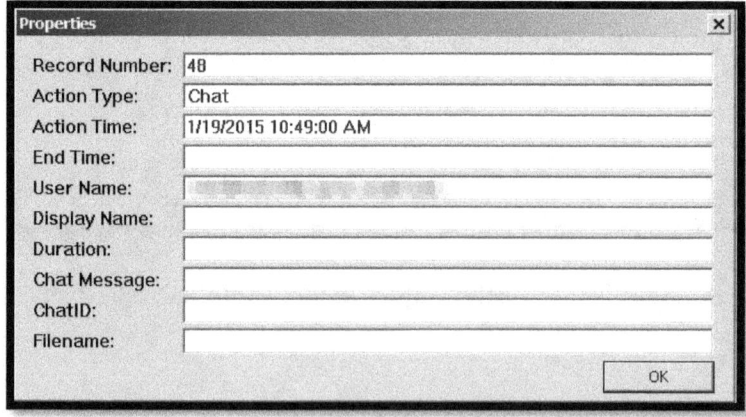

Individual or bulk messages can be exported as text files but this method results in a messy presentation. To easily view all the relevant Skype conversations select **View** and **HTML Report – All Items**.

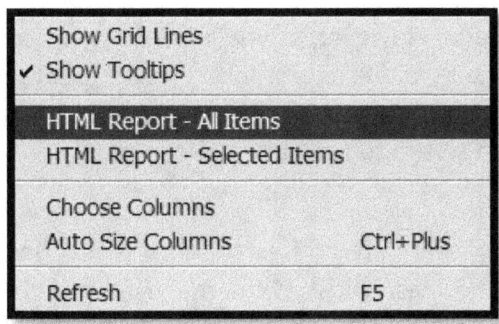

This brings up all of the data in an easy to read configuration. However, it does require opening up an internet browser to view. If the Skype log is being viewed on a suspect's computer it may be best to copy the log file using the steps outlined previously and then view the messages on another computer.

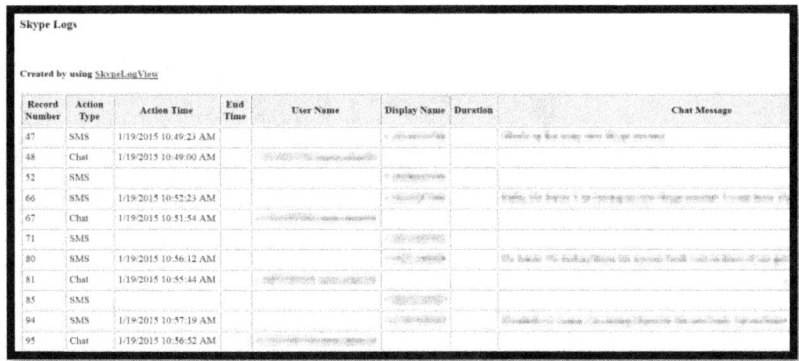

The resulting HTML file can be saved and/or converted to a PDF file for inclusion with a police report.

For investigators who are looking for an economical, single purpose tool for recovering and analyzing Skype files, Sanderson Forensics develops and sells SkypeAlyzer. In addition to the functionality found in SkypeLogView, SkypAlyzer can recover deleted messages and conversations. Priced at $260.00 it is a credible forensic option. However, if you are going to spend departmental money I would suggest looking at their SQLite Forensic Toolkit. It's a little more expensive at $495.00 but it can parse other types of SQLite databases from computers and mobile devices.

Unfortunately, there are no free tools for recovering Skype files from mobile devices. Most of the major forensic tools such as those developed by Cellebrite, Microsystemation, and Oxygen Forensics have the capability to recover Skype contacts, messages, and log files.

Legal Requirements

In most cases Skype requires a legal demand before turning over any information. However, there is an exception to this in situations involving exigent circumstances. Exigent circumstances involve imminent threat of serious bodily injury or death to a person. Examples of exigent circumstances include suicidal subjects, abductions and kidnappings, missing persons, and hostage situation. Skype will provide information necessary to investigate cases involving exigent circumstances without a subpoena, search warrant, or court order.

There is a misperception in the law enforcement community that the mere statement by a police officer of exigent circumstances is sufficient to compel disclosure by Skype. This is not the case. Skype, and any other provider, must have a good faith belief exigent circumstances exist before providing information. It may be necessary to provide Skype some details of the situation in order to obtain their cooperation. This does not mean Skype's representatives need to be given all of the details of the case. It is sufficient to provide them with relevant facts and circumstances supporting the belief there is an imminent threat and Skype possesses information relevant and material to the efforts of law enforcement to prevent the loss of life or serious bodily injury.

Many providers will release the information with a condition the requesting law enforcement officer provides a search warrant, court order, or subpoena within 48 hours after the data was provided. There is no statutory requirement to do so. However, it is a recommended practice to obtain an after the fact legal demand to protect evidence obtained during the investigation. This is particularly true with Skype. Skype retains message, voice, and video content. This type of information typically requires a search warrant to obtain. It is not uncommon for information obtained during an exigent circumstances request to generate evidence of other criminal activity. Law enforcement officers

31

who desire to use this evidence in a separate criminal investigation would be well advised to routinely obtain an *ex-post facto*, or after the fact, legal demand to prevent later attempts to suppress that evidence by a defense attorney. Even though information obtained during an exigent circumstances request is routinely admitted into evidence in criminal proceedings it makes no sense to give a defense attorney the opportunity to litigate the matter. Obtaining a search warrant after the fact effectively closes the door on suppression motions.

SWATting Incidents Involving Skype and How to Investigate Them

It is not uncommon for Skype's trunked phone numbers to be involved in harassment or SWATting incidents. For those that have not experienced a SWATting incident it usually involves a suspect calling the police to report an incident likely to evoke a large response and/or the deployment of a tactical team. These have included active shooter situations at schools, bomb threats at court houses, and barricaded suspect situations at the homes of celebrities.

If the calling phone number is one of Skype's outgoing trunk numbers such as 661-748-0240 or 661-748-0241 it is possible to identify the account and account holder information used to make the call. In order to research the relevant call Skype needs an appropriate legal demand or exigent circumstances to perform what is known as a calls to destination search, sometimes referred to in the telecommunications industry as a specialized records search. This type of search works not only for Skype but for any telecommunications company involving a caller ID blocked or unknown phone number.

A calls to destination search directs the provider to search their records for all calls made to a certain number. In order to be successful this requires providing Skype with the victim or target's phone number, the date the call was received, and the time the call was received. The time element is crucial for the success of a calls to destination search. Many phone lines, such as the main phone number for a school or court receive hundreds and even thousands of phone calls a day. A narrow time frame allows Skype to search their records and avoids the investigator being inundated with multiple numbers requiring follow-up. If the victim or witness is unsure of the exact time a threatening phone call was received an investigator should attempt to narrow the window down to a five or ten minute time frame. Skype also requires the approximate duration of the call. An often missed element in calls to destination searches is providing Skype, or any other provider, the time zone the call occurred in. The following is sample language that can be incorporated into an investigation involving Skype, or any other communications service, o perform a calls to destination search.

Provider shall conduct a calls-to-destination search of ###### (Provider's) call detain records (CDRs) to identify the telephone number(s) of any and all ###### (Provider's) customers that called one or more of the following numbers: 555-555-1212, 415-555-1212, during the period #####(date) to ##### (date). Provider shall also provide the then-current subscriber information for any telephone number(s) so identified.

Subscriber information is to include billing address, subscriber name, account number, Social Security Number, driver license number, date of birth, alternate contact numbers given by the subscriber, dates of service, and any associated equipment information such as Electronic Serial Number (ESN), International Mobile Equipment Identifier/Identification (IMEI), and/or International Mobile Subscriber Information (IMSI), customer service notes recorded in the account, and billing information for the specified number.

Legal Process

Absent exigent circumstances, obtaining information from Skype is going to involve submitting a legal demand. One of the first issues that perplexes many judges and law enforcement officers is the location for service of process for Skype in Luxembourg.

Prior to being acquired by Microsoft, Skype established itself in Luxembourg. The company's subpoena compliance operations have not been consolidated with the main group at Microsoft. This creates an issue for some investigators and magistrates who wonder what their authority is to demand records from a foreign country related to an investigation in the United States.

Luxembourg and the United States entered into a Mutual Legal Assistance Treaty (MLAT) in 1997 that became effective in 2001. Article 15 Paragraph 1 of that treaty addresses the issue of international searches and states:

> *The Requested State shall execute a request requiring search, seizure, and transfer of any item to the Requesting State if:*
>
> *a) a judicial authority of the Requesting State issues, approves, or otherwise authorizes the request; and*
>
> *b) the request includes the information justifying such action under the laws of the Requested State.*
>
> *For purposes of this paragraph, a judicial authority shall be, as appropriate, a prosecutor, court, or examining magistrate.*

The full text of the treaty can be found at the State Department http://www.state.gov/documents/organization/76194.pdf

Skype routinely responds to judicial orders from courts in the United States without invoking any international law enforcement or judicial bodies.

Skype Service of Process Information

Search warrants, court order, or subpoenas should be addressed to:

Skype Communications SARL
23-29 Rives de Clausen, L-2165 Luxembourg

Legal demands can be sent via email to:
lerm@skype.net

Legal demands can be sent via fax to:
+352 26 20 15 82

Skype does not publicize any phone numbers for their subpoena compliance division. In a case involving exigent circumstances, email a request to LEALERT@microsoft.com. The subject line should read "Urgent Skype Request." The Microsoft law enforcement team will forward the request to Skype in Luxembourg for processing.

Preservation Letters

Skype routinely preserves voice, text, and video messages sent over their service for between 30 and 90 days depending on the type of message. Despite this, it is a good practice to send a preservation letter any time there is an investigation involving Skype.

A preservation letter is simply a request on departmental letterhead asking Skype, or any other internet, email, or cellular service provider, to preserve information in their possession while an investigator seeks a search warrant, court order, or subpoena. In light of Skype's existing preservation practices it may seem an unnecessary step. However, for those investigators with large caseloads, submission of a preservation letter insures the necessary evidence will be still exist by the time an appropriate legal demand is obtained and served.

Most states do not have a criminal or penal code section authorizing preservation letters. The statutory authority for obtaining a preservation letter is found is federal law; specifically Title 18 United States Code Section 2703(f) which reads:

> *(f) Requirement To Preserve Evidence.—*
> *(1) In general.-A provider of wire or electronic communication services or a remote computing service, upon the request of a governmental entity, shall take all necessary steps to preserve records and other evidence in its possession pending the issuance of a court order or other process.*
> *(2) Period of retention.-Records referred to in paragraph (1) shall be retained for a period of 90 days, which shall be extended for an additional 90-day period upon a renewed request by the governmental entity.*

Submitting a preservation letter buys a law enforcement officer 90 days initially and can be extended one time for an additional 90 days.

Preservation letters do not require judicial authorization or a supervisor's signature. Any law enforcement officer may submit one. Departmental letterhead, submission from a .gov email address, or using a specialized law enforcement portal prevent unauthorized people from submitting preservation requests.

While Skype does not have a policy of notifying customers of receipt of a preservation letter it is still a good practice to include a non-disclosure statement in the letter.

Preservation letters can be customized based on the needs of the investigation. The following is a good template to start with.

Sample Preservation Letter

You are hereby requested to preserve, under the provisions of Title 18, United States Code, Section 2703(f)(1), the following records in your custody or control, including records stored on backup media:

> A. All stored electronic communications and other files controlled by user accounts owned by _____(suspect name)/associated_____ (suspect Skype number.)
> B. Registration Details
> C. Billing Address
> D. Skype Online Current Subscription
> E. Purchase History
> F. Skype Out Records
> G. Skype Online Records
> H. SMS Records
> I. Skype WiFi Records
> J. E-mail & Password Records
> K Any other records related to the above-referenced names and user names, including, without limitation, correspondence, billing records, records of contact by any person or entity about the above-referenced names and user names, and any other subscriber information.

You are requested to preserve for a period of 90 days the records described above currently in your possession. This request applies only retrospectively; it does not obligate you to capture and preserve new information that arises after the date of this request. Failure to comply with this request could subject you to liability under 18 U.S.C. § 2707.

You also are requested not to disclose the existence of this request to the subscriber or any other person, other than as necessary to comply with this request.

Please refer any questions to _____. Thank you for your cooperation.

Subpoena

Some law enforcement agencies, particularly Federal, are addicted to administrative subpoenas. Unfortunately, this addiction can be problematic when dealing with Skype. As a general rule content, such as the text, video, and voice messages retained by Skype, require a search warrant to obtain. Investigating officers or agents who use a subpoena typically only receive subscriber information and transactional data. Unfortunately, the use of a subpoena deprives them of the rare opportunity to obtain communications content available via other means. Subpoenas may be useful during the initial stages of an investigation. But, when dealing with Skype, the content in their possession makes the added effort to obtain a search warrant worth it.

Court Order

Many law enforcement agencies use court orders obtained pursuant to Federal law. Title 18 United States Code Section 2703(d) allows state and local judges to issue an order for the production of records. This section is often used because it only requires "reasonable grounds to believe... the records or other information sought, are relevant and material to an ongoing criminal investigation." As this section does not require probable cause to obtain records it is commonly used to obtain information. This is especially true in investigations when there is evidence of criminal activity but it does not rise to the probable cause threshold.

Similar to search warrants, court orders do not justify obtaining content from Skype such as messages and videos. While 18 USC 2703(d) is a very helpful statute, it should not be used in circumstances where the actual Skype messages are pertinent to the investigation.

Search Warrant

Search warrants are the best option for obtaining information from Skype. However, they need to be detailed enough to obtain the relevant information without being overly broad. Each item of Skype information to be seized needs to be supported in the Affidavit. Simply putting the phrase "any and all information" is a bad practice as this language has consistently been found to be unconstitutionally vague as it fails to meet the reasonable particularity requirement of the Fourth Amendment.

The first step in drafting a search warrant affidavit is to properly identify the Skype account or parameters Skype uses to search for accounts. The first method of identification is the Skype ID. This is the specific account username that is visible to those who participate or receive a Skype call or message. Skype can also identify accounts based on the Skype Online Number. Skype Online numbers can be either international or US based.

As noted in the previous section on SWATting and harassing phone calls, Skype can search for any of their customers who called a cellular or landline number if the investigating officer provides the receiving number, date, time, and duration of the phone call. Skype can also search for their customers based on their 16 digit credit card number. This method of searching can be particularly useful when a Skype application is discovered to be on or associated with a mobile device such as during a forensic examination. While some information can be recovered from a device, the company has additional information such as the stored messages and videos that may be relevant.

Search warrants should be tailored to recover information relevant to the investigation. Skype's legal division states the following information is available with a legal demand.

- Registration Details-This includes information captured at the time the account was registered. This may include identification data such as name, username, address, telephone number, mobile number, email address, and profile information such as age, gender, country of residence, language preference and any user profile information.
- Billing Address-The user provided billing address used in conjunction with payment for Skype services.
- Skype Online Current Subscription List-A list of Skype users currently subscribed to by the suspect.
- Purchase History-Financial transactions with Skype including method of payment information and billing address.
- Skype Out Records-Historical call detail records for calls placed to cellular and landline phone numbers. [NOTE: These records are maintained by Skype for six month. However, records beyond six months may reside on the target's computer or mobile devices used to access Skype.]
- Skype Online Records-Historical call detail records for calls placed to the Skype number from landline and mobile numbers. [NOTE: These records are maintained by Skype for six month. However, records beyond six months may reside on the target's computer or mobile devices used to access Skype.]

- Short Message System (SMS) Records-Text messages including the content of the message. [NOTE: These records are maintained by Skype for six month. However, records beyond six months may reside on the target's computer or mobile devices used to access Skype.]

Calls and messages between Skype users do NOT generate call detail records. However, these records may be recovered from the target's computer or mobile device used to access Skype.

- Skype Wi-Fi Records-Historical records of connection to Skype Wi-Fi access points. [NOTE: These records are maintained by Skype for six month. However, records beyond six months may reside on the target's computer or mobile devices used to access Skype.]
- Email and Password Records-A historical record of emails and password change activity.

Other Retained Data Not Publicly Disclosed By Skype

Skype retains additional information that is not readily disclosed by their subpoena compliance group. Skype reveals they collect and retain this data in their privacy policy but fail to note it in their subpoena compliance documentation. This includes:

- System Information such as computer platform and operating system
- Mobile device information such as device type, manufacturer name, model number, operating system, and cellular service provider.
- Contact imported from email and social media accounts
- Content of instant messages, voice messages, and video messages.
- Location information provided by the customer to access Wi-Fi access points or shared by the user with another Skype customer. This may include historical GPS location data.
- Associated social media accounts such as Facebook, LinkedIn, or Twitter.
- Linked Microsoft accounts.

Sample Search Warrant Language

The following are suggested language for specific items in a Skype search warrant. It may be modified or adapted based on the needs of the investigating officer's jurisdiction.

Sample Affidavit In Support Of Search Warrant

I, [[OFFICER NAME]], being first duly sworn, hereby depose and state as follows:

INTRODUCTION AND OFFICER BACKGROUND

1. I make this affidavit in support of an application for a search warrant for information associated with certain Skype accounts that is stored at premises owned, maintained, controlled, or operated by Skype, a communications company owned by Microsoft but headquartered separately in Luxembourg. The information to be searched is described in the following paragraphs and in Attachment A. This affidavit is made in support of an application for a search warrant under California Penal Code § 1524(a)(7) and Title 18 United States Code § 2703(d) to require Skype to disclose to the investigating officer records and other information in its possession, pertaining to the subscriber or customer using the service.

2. I am a [INSERT RANK/POSITION] with the [[AGENCY]], and have been since [[DATE]]. [[DESCRIBE TRAINING AND EXPERIENCE TO THE EXTENT IT SHOWS QUALIFICATION TO SPEAK ABOUT THE INTERNET AND OTHER TECHNICAL MATTERS]].

3. The facts in this affidavit come from my personal observations, my training and experience, and information obtained from other agents and witnesses. This affidavit is intended to show merely that there is sufficient probable cause for the requested warrant and does not set forth all of my knowledge about this matter.

4. Based on my training and experience and the facts as set forth in this affidavit, there is probable cause to believe that violations of [[STATUTES]] have been committed by [[SUSPECTS or unknown persons]]. There is also probable cause to search the information described in Attachment A for evidence of these crimes [[and contraband or fruits of these crimes]], as described in Attachment B.

PROBABLE CAUSE

5. [[Give facts establishing probable cause. At a minimum, establish a connection between the Skype account and a suspected crime; mention whether a preservation request was sent (or other facts suggesting Skype still has the records desired)]]

6. Skype owns and operates a communications service that transmits voice calls, video, and messages over the internet. Skype users can make and receive local, long distance, and international phones calls, participate in video chat or conversations or send and receive video messages, send and receive short message system (SMS) text messages, and send and receive electronic files including documents, pictures, audio, and video.

7. Skype may be installed and used on a desktop or laptop computer, tablet, or mobile phone including those using operating systems from Apple, Blackberry, Google, and Windows.

8. Skype requires users to provide basic contact information to the company during the registration process. This information may include identification data such as name, username, address, telephone number, mobile number, email address, and profile information such as age, gender, country of residence, and language preference. and any user profile information.

9. Skype users can elect to make public profile information consisting of images, links to personal web pages, and links to social media web sites.

10. Skype users may subscribe to other Skype users with whom they are interested or associated.

11. When communicating with non-Skype users the company keeps transaction records during the normal course of business commonly referred to as call detail records that consist of the date, time, sender, receiver, duration, and content of phone calls, text messages, and video messages. According to the company, the transactional records are maintained for six months and data files are stored for 30 to 90 days depending on the type of file.

12. In order to use Skype a customer must either purchasing credits and agree to a monthly or otherwise recurring payment option. This necessitates either providing the company with credit card information, including name, billing address, and credit card number, or the use of an online payment processor such as PayPal.

13. Skype retains system information about the types of devices a customer uses to access their service. This can include computer platform and operating system, internet protocol (IP) address information, and mobile device information such as device type, manufacturer name, model number, operating system, and cellular service provider.

14. Skype users may elect to import their contacts from email and social media accounts. This contact information can include name, email address, and/or phone numbers.

15. Skype accesses and stores location information regarding their customers. The location information includes Wi-Fi access points when a customer uses Skype from a home or free Wi-Fi spot, global positioning system (GPS) data when a user searches for free Skype Wi-Fi access points, and GPS data when a Skype user shares their location with another user.

16. Skype users can link their social media accounts with the communication provider. These social media accounts may include Facebook, LinkedIn, and Twitter.

17. Skype users may have an associated Microsoft account and other services. These associated services may include online file storage, Microsoft email services, and/or other Microsoft products or services.

18. Skype also retains Internet Protocol ("IP") logs for a given user ID or IP address. These logs may contain information about the actions taken by the user ID or IP address on Skype, including information about the type of action, the date and time of the action, and the user ID and IP address associated with the action.

19. Skype uses the following terms to describe the data in their possession:

Registration Details-This includes information captured at the time the account was registered. This may include identification data such as name, username, address, telephone number, mobile number, email address, and profile information such as age, gender, country of residence, language preference and any user profile information.

Billing Address-The user provided billing address used in conjunction with payment for Skype services.

Skype Online Current Subscription List-A list of Skype users currently subscribed to by the suspect.

Purchase History-Financial transactions with Skype including method of payment information and billing address.

Skype Out Records-Historical call detail records for calls placed to cellular and landline phone numbers.

Skype Online Records-Historical call detail records for calls placed to the Skype number from landline and mobile numbers.

Short Message System (SMS) Records-Text messages including the content of the message.

Skype Wi-Fi Records-Historical records of connection to Skype Wi-Fi access points.

Email and Password Records-A historical record of emails and password change activity.

20.   Communication providers like Skype typically retain additional information about their users' accounts during the normal course of business, such as information about the length of service (including start date), the types of service utilized, and the means and source of any payments associated with the service (including any credit card or bank account number). In some cases, Skype users may communicate directly with Skype about issues relating to their account, such as technical problems, billing inquiries, or complaints from other users. Providers like Facebook typically retain records about such communications, including records of contacts between the user and the provider's support services, as well records of any actions taken by the provider or user as a result of the communications.

21.   Therefore, the computers of Skype are likely to contain all the material just described, including stored electronic communications and information concerning subscribers and their use of Skype, such as account access information, transaction information, and account application.

INFORMATION TO BE SEARCHED AND THINGS TO BE SEIZED

22.   I anticipate executing this warrant under the California Penal Code, specifically § 1524(a)(7), and Title 18 United States

Code § 2703(d) by using the warrant to require Skype to disclose to the government copies of the records and other information, including the content of communications, particularly described in Section I of Attachment B.

CONCLUSION

23.   Based on the forgoing, I request that the Court issue the proposed search warrant.

24.   This Court has jurisdiction to issue the requested warrant because it is "a court of competent jurisdiction" as defined by 18 U.S.C. § 2711. Specifically, 18 U.S.C. § 2711 (B) a court of general criminal jurisdiction of a State authorized by law of that State to issue search warrants.

REQUEST FOR SEALING

25.   These documents discuss an ongoing criminal investigation that is neither public nor known to all of the targets of the investigation. Accordingly, there is good cause to seal these documents because their premature disclosure may seriously jeopardize that investigation.

REQUEST FOR NON-DISCLOSURE

26.   I am aware Skype may notify the subscriber of receipt of a search warrant unless they are specifically prohibited from doing so by the issuing judge. Disclosure of the existence of a search warrant would seriously jeopardize the on-going investigation. Accordingly, I request Skype, it's employees and agents, be prohibited from notifying their customer, nor anyone else not directly involved in satisfying the requirements of the search warrant, until further order of the Court.

Respectfully submitted,

[[OFFICER NAME[]

[OFFICER POSITION OR TITLE]

[[AGENCY]]

Subscribed and sworn to before me on
_____, 201___

_____

SUPERIOR COURT JUDGE

Free Skype Search Warrant Template

A digital format of the preservation letter and search warrant language can be obtained for FREE from https://gumroad.com/cipublishing. Simply select the appropriate template and put $0 in the checkout box and the files can be downloaded to your computer.

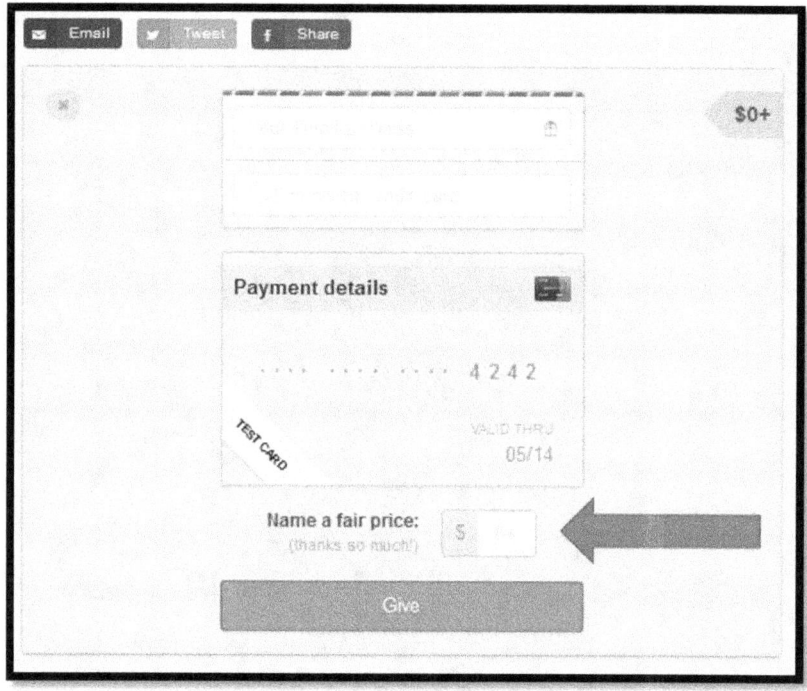

You might also be interested in:

ONLINE INVESTIGATIONS: Craigslist

How to find narcotics, human trafficking, explosives, stolen military equipment, fencing operations and more using specific keywords and search terms

Undercover operations: Tools and techniques for effective operations

Downloadable search warrant templates tem-

ONLINE INVESTIGATIONS: Facebook

What kind of information does Facebook have? How long do they keep it? Is deleted or deactivated account information still available?

A downloadable Facebook search warrant template

FREE tools for recovering Facebook passwords and downloading profiles

ONLINE INVESTIGATIONS: Snapchat

Are the messages really gone? A detailed guide to the information the company collects and retains and how to obtain it

Snapchat and mobile device search warrants to forensically recover Snapchat messages and log files.